Somewhere Between Massachusetts and San Pedro

Vincent Wallace

BookLeaf Publishing

Presentation by *BookLeaf Publishing*

Web: www.bookleafpub.com

E-mail: info@bookleafpub.com

ISBN: 9789357440318

First edition 2023

For my parents

For always pushing me to follow my dreams

ACKNOWLEDGEMENT

I would like to thank all of my former English teachers for inspiring to become a better writer. Mrs. Richter, Mr. Hoffman, Mrs. Hoffman, Ms. Davis, and Mr. Dawson. Special thanks go to the English teachers in my home life, my mom and grandma, as well anyone who ever bought or gave me a book of poetry...I promise your gift did not go to waste.

PREFACE

I first started writing poetry when I was a senior in high school. I had bought myself a beautiful leather-bound journal so I could jot down my thoughts. Both coming out of the coronavirus pandemic and preparing for post-graduation life was beginning to take its toll on me. I was constantly stressed out, and I thought getting my thoughts out of my head and onto paper might help me to organize my brain a bit better. It did, and then one day I sat down in the living room before I had to leave for school, and I penned my first poem. I don't know what made me do it, but the words sort of just came to me. It was about journaling by the fireplace before you have to leave in the morning…creative huh?

As remarkably unoriginal as my first work was, I was ecstatic. I had never written anything like that before, and it did seem to have a nice flow to it when I read it back to myself. I started writing more poems here and there, and I realized that they helped me calm down more than anything. Poetry was not only fun and challenging, but it was also therapeutic. I began to dive into the readings of the old greats and make my poems longer and more complicated.

Eventually I decided to just make that leather bound my poetry journal. It still is.

When I sat down to write this book, I didn't know exactly how to begin. Most poetry books feature some kind of theme, even if it's a loose one. What could I write 21 poems about? I kept thinking to myself. What do I know and understand that deeply? After a bit of thinking, I came to realize there was really only one answer…my home.

I have lived in Fort Wayne, Indiana my entire life. Since I was 11, I have lived on about three and a half acres out in the country. I wouldn't want to live anywhere else. I realized if there was anything I could write that much material about, it was my hometown. I picked up the computer and away I went.

The title of the book is in reference to where Fort Wayne lies in the US. I live close to the Old Lincoln Highway, which was the first road to run all the way from the east to the west coast in the country's history. I'm smack dab in the middle of it. It's also a tribute to my two poetry heroes; Robert Frost and Charles Bukowski.

Frost was a former farmer and teacher before he made his living as a poet. Although he was born in San Francisco, he spent almost all of his life in New England. He was well-read, well-spoken, and generally well-liked. Bukowski was an alcoholic drifter who worked about a thousand different jobs before writing full-time. He was a notorious asshole who didn't much care for the likes of Frost or Whittman. He felt they were simply full of it.

I love both of them so much. I think many of us like to think that we are Frost. We are dignified, respectable, and admirable by the standards of our society. Sometimes however, we are really Bukowski. We're Frost when we prepare a delicious meal for our family, and all eat at the table and hold hands to pray. What a lovely image. However, we are all certainly Bukowski's behind the wheel of a car in downtown traffic, or when we find out one of our coworkers has been gossiping about us behind our backs. Some of the language that can be heard in those scenarios would likely give Ol' Frost a heart attack…and Bukowski would probably laugh so hard he'd keel over and hold his stomach.

These poems are my best interpretation of balancing those two in my mind, as well as paying due homage to the place that has made me who I am. I know that I am not exactly a poet laureate, and I'm probably a long shot from being on any kind of New York Times lists, but I can promise you this; this is me. This is about as authentic as it gets with me, and I just hope that maybe somewhere somebody will pick this up…maybe someone who dealt with some of the same stuff I did…and it will make them feel a bit better. Maybe even make them love poetry the way Frost and Bukowski did for me. Not that I am them, but you get the idea.

Anyway, I'll quit being cheesy and let you get to what you came for, the poems.

Happy reading and thank you for giving me a chance.

-Vincent Wallace

What Else Would I Do?

My mom is a teacher
She's been one my entire life
and probably will be for the rest of hers
even if not professionally
I once asked her why
Why choose a thankless job
with low pay and an early wakeup call
She simply said
"It's what I love to do!"
Adding always
"What else would I do?"

Once I asked my father about retirement
I asked if he had any plans to
when he got older
"No,"
He said
"I don't think I ever quite will retire."
I was stunned
I knew his job wasn't exactly his favorite
but I couldn't fathom the idea of a man
never enjoying the leisure of retirement
I said in surprise
"Why?!"
He simply said

"What else would I do?
I hate sitting around all day
like some useless old fart
I wanna do something!"

Now I have an answer for when
I am asked why I teach
and why I'll always teach

What else would I do?

Just South of Lincoln's Highway

Just South of Lincoln's Highway
Where neighborhoods die down
Just happens to be the place
where I tend to hang around

Looming large is quiet while
Small and quaint is my abode
A 3 acre American dream
Just two hundred yards offroad

Surrounded by the fields
Of farmers lost and oft' forgotten
Of centuries of planters
Growing corn and beans and cotton

Heating up the home
Is the fireplace's roar
Complemented by the cracking
And the creaking of wood floors

The bookshelves lined with classics
Bronte and Twain galore
While Frost and Wittman argue
If Silversteins a bore

The shelves prized possession
Is the Bible holding court
To be evermore consulted
When one seems out of sorts

The records and the dancers spin
While Sinatra softly croons
And a lady smiles politely
As her husband softly swoons

And there's old me
Wondering how I'll still keep on
Because in the wild world ahead
I feel somewhat like a pawn

So if I'm ever missing
If I'm nowhere to be found
Just South of Ole' Abe's highway
Is where I hang around.

Midnight Hauntings

After the early dusk
of winter
Sets upon the Indiana countryside
The ghosts of dwellers past
descend to the earth

The ghosts of the Miami
of Kekionga
The ghost of Little Turtle
shooting arrows across the woodlands
left to be found for future pilgrims
The ghost of Mad Anthony Wayne
marching into the Northwest Territory
just as he had years before for the Revolution
in the name of Washington

It hides in the old fort
among the old cabins and fireplaces.
Keeping the army warm from the blizzards
that often terrorize the Union men
just as it terrorizes the wigwams
of the chilly natives
Toughing it out through yet another harsh winter
In search of food
Game to hunt

They tell stories
Stories of their past
Stories of their ancestral
sister and brothers
Just as Mad Anthony and his soldiers tell stories
of their fallen brothers
Generals of old
who like them fought in the name of Washington

Much appears after the early dusk
of winter
Sets upon the Indiana countryside

Heaven Pierces Through

For the
laborers making their
way home
after sweat filled days
of toil and strife
Heaven pierces through

For the
farmer hoping for fuel
to aid his
crop in flourishing
so that he may feed his family
Heaven pierces through

Like angels
playing harps and drums
to announce the arrival of a new
and brighter season
of life
Like Saint Peter
raising his staff
at the gates of paradise
announcing the arrival
of a new soul
to live among the alive

Heaven Pierces through
clouds of a chilly Wednesday afternoon

For the young teacher
shaken from an unexpected
first day
needing the reassurance from God
Oh, how heaven pierces through

Me and My Sitcoms

Why do I watch sitcoms
that are 30 years old…at least
Why instead of gaming with friends
or watching football
do I set myself down in front of the TV
And watch reruns of
Everybody Loves Raymond
or
The Andy Griffith Show

These are the type of questions I get asked
when my mother
or my friends
or my sister and brother
see sit town and flip on the television
I'll tell you why

Because no therapy
will ever have the effect
on me
that a strong willed and honest
Andy Taylor pep talk will have
The way Mayberry's finest citizen
always seem to keep his composure
is one of the most

inspiring things
I have ever witnessed

Because the simplicity
of watching the sheriff
slowly walk that beautiful woman
up to her porch
with nothing but the most noble of intentions
always has and always will remind my heart to
stay strong

Because the hilarity
of watching two brothers
who could not be more
different from one another
or more different from their father
try and make sense of this ridiculous thing we
call
Family
Tickles me right in my gut
just as the hilarity of living it
with my own brother
does

So people
instead of moaning about
how I waste my time
and watching these shows isn't any fun
maybe take a minute stop

and
listen
to the sheriff’s whistle
as he walks his young boy down to the fishing
hole
or
listen
as the exhausted father rakes up
his children's autumn mess
from the afternoon

You may begin to see, dear reader, what it is I’m
talking about
but until then
Leave me and my sitcoms the hell alone

Car Window Frost

Many a mornings
I have awoken
to a sight so bleak
My heart was nearly broken

It's a sight that's terrorized
The hearts of the Midwest
since automobiles
were first put to the test

The sight isn't gas
leaking out from my tank
or my old engine growling
And shooting off blanks

It's a sight that, ironically
robs me of view
Why it's ice on my windshield
and back window too

I'm don't quite no why
or how it became
considering last night
featured no freezing rain

But I do suppose
to think it is fair
That it simply derives
from the freezing of air

Nevertheless
I give winter no pass
As I arm myself with scraper
and viciously attack the glass

Eventually, of course
the battle comes to a close
and the saga of car window frost
is left only for my prose

The Way Things Creak at Night

12:30 AM
I pull into the driveway
the gravel driveway rustling
beneath my tire
It's been a long night

I whip my car into its usual spot
and slowly pull myself
out of the front seat
As I step out
the sound of my feet
shifting the earth below me
is much louder than usual
Almost like its trying to tell me something

It talks to me until I reach the house
I get reach for the door handle
and slowly let it open with a loud cackle
ricocheting throughout the house
almost waking my family

One step inside and
crack
crack

crack
goes the wooden floor
as if Poe's beating heart buried within
reminding me of my great sin
against myself
my loved ones
My God

I cherish the day time
No one to guilt me for hours on end

A Classroom Out of Hibernation

No longer does the darkness
engulf the aimless desk
or blacken all the posters
when lights clicked to rest

No longer do the blinds
that for months concealed the day
rob me off my joy
for now I swing them away

No longer do the students
sit around and twiddle thumbs
for now they may awaken
their sense once left dumb

No longer I sit and wait
for life to start again
Tis now the time for learners
like you and me to leap ahead

Quit Daydreaming? Why?

"Quit Daydreaming!"
said my mother
as I sat at the dinner table
fantasizing about dinosaurs
or cars and planes
or animals
"Eat your food!" she'd shout
There was never any time
for Tyrannosaurus Rex's
or monster truck rallies
in my mind
not when there was food to be eaten

"Quit Daydreaming!"
said my teacher
as I sat at my desk
pondering on how fast I could
drive if both me and my best friend Johnny
slammed our feet onto the gas pedal;
a very interesting an nuanced question
we thought
"What's the answer?" she'd hiss
What did it matter
that me and Johnny and I
had just come up with a question so engaging

as well as a task so daunting
that it would take years to answer
Why bother with that when there's times tables
to learn
Ms. Bee always said

"Quit Daydreaming!"
said my boss
as I sat back to ponder
how glorious it must feel
to topple everest
and claim my spot amongst the legends
climbing lore
"Get to work!" he'd growl
no matter that I was on a quest
to achieve
what so few men had ever achieved
and placing my name
within the vernacular of the human memory
No sense in thinking about that
when there is endless scrolling
and typing to be done.

But why?
Why give up on
the dreams and imagination
of the mind?
Why take this God given gift and right '
for granted to the extent

that we ridicule one another for having
aspirations?
I say no more!

No more
shouting or hissing or growling
at those who wish to explore
No more
hatred for the children
who simply wish to tickle their brain
with tales of whimsy and wonder

Quit Daydreaming?

Never!

The Days That Felt Like Adventure

"So you left, huh?"
"Yeah…yeah I did. Three months ago today."
"What sparked that decision?"
"A lot of things."
"Very specific I see."
"Well, that's all there is to it."
"If you say so."
We drove quietly for another ten or twelve miles
I can't remember which
I pondered on what he'd said
"That's all there is to it."
A tell-tale sign that there is a lot more to it.
I'd never known him to be a quitter of any kind…even when he should be
Hell, hadn't he been the one to try out for the basketball team in high school even though he could never even crack it in junior high?
He'd made it to
I guess that was before life got in the way of his work ethic

Why in the hell was it his business why I'd left.

I had my reasons and I was happy with my decision…besides…it's not like he would understand.
Than again, I wasn't sure I did
"You hungry?"
"Kinda."
"What are you feelin'?"
"Something edible."
"What the hell's your problem!?"
"Chill out dude, damn. I was joking."
"Sorry."
Why the hell did he have to be so vague all the time?
All he had to say was whether he wanted a damn burger
Was that so hard?
What's his deal?
Normally he found that hysterical
It felt like an hour before we spoke again
"You know dude…you can talk to me."
"You can too pal."
"No dipshit, I mean you can like…TALK to me.
If something is bothering you.
"I know dude, thanks."
"Do you?"
I thought I did
Maybe not
I just wish he would listen

I wouldn’t ask about his personal life if I didn’t care
He’s like my brother
Another thirty minutes before I heard anything
Worth the wait
Three times over
“I had never been in that bad of shape in my life.”
“I wouldn’t beat yourself up too bad over that.
A lot of college kids gain weight their first year or two.”
“That’s not what I meant.”
It took me a second, but I figured it out.
“Lemme ask you something.”
“Shoot.”
“Have you ever laid in your bed
for hours on end
for no other reason than the fact that
you had no motivation to do anything else?
I mean have you ever struggled
to work up the courage to do something
as simple as laundry?
“Well…I mean I guess…”
“You don’t need to bullshit me.”
A long sigh
“I haven’t ever felt that way, man.”
“Be happy. Thank God even.”
“That bad, huh?”
A long pause.

“I wouldn’t wish that shit on anyone but the
devil himself.”
I never knew anyone could be in such bad shape
Especially not someone
like him
“I would lay there
and just stare at my ceiling fan until I got
nauseous
than I would stare at my phone until my eyes
started to hurt
than I would listen to music off my phone until
no good songs were left
than it was back to the ceiling fan…that fucking
ceiling fan.”

“Damn, dude.
Why didn’t you ever tell anyone?
At least not for so long.”
“Would you tell someone?”
“I mean…I would think so.”
“Don’t we all”
Almost home
forty-five minutes later
we’d made it.
I wasn’t quite sure what to say
Three and half hours of driving
To much McDonalds
and a hell of a deep conversation

I sure didn't plan on sharing that
I guess if I was going too
he would've been the guy
I hope I wasn't to hard on him
I'm just a little tired of people asking at this point
Silence as we arrive
Silence as we park
Silence as he we open the doors
I can't help myself
Maybe the outside gave me a little more courage
"Do you ever miss it?"
"Sometimes."
"C'mon, dude.
We've come this far."
A long sigh

"I miss the days that felt like adventures."
There it is
"Days when the campus felt like
something out of a novel.
Every street and sidewalk
felt like the yellow brick road
I would explore that square mile
like I was a Spanish conquistador
Looking for gold
I would go to basketball games
in the arena of my dreams
watch the team of my childhood

wage war with the whole conference
Once, I even played on it
I ran the same floor
That once graced the likes of
Damon Bailey and Kent Benson
That kinda shit
That's what I miss."
"Then why in the hell ever leave?"
"Adventure didn't come around all that often.
Hell showed its face just about every day, and
one day of adventure isn't worth a month of hell
That's for sure."
I had to chuckle
"Who are you, Confucius?"
"Something like that, I guess. I think I'm just
relieved I'm back."
"You and me both."

I Don't Much Go for City Roads

I don’t much go for city roads
Never have, and probably never will

Packed streets downtown
with so little room
and so many people vying for spots on road
going God knows where for God knows what

Maybe only God knows

Cities like Chicago
Philadelphia
Boston
never much suited me
Don’t mistake me
Of course I could explore the wonders
of the history of those towns for hours and days
on end

But that's the sidewalks and buildings
not the roads

No, I prefer country roads
Wide open with no one else for miles ahead

or behind
Acres of farmland
with churches and houses sprinkled in on top
While livestock and horses roam the ranches
annoyed by the chickens and roosters constant
babbling

No, I don't go much for city roads
and I'll be damned if I ever do.

Exhaustion

Out of breath
Out of shape
Out of bed

A few recurring themes in my life
Don’t mistake me
I love what I do
The teaching
learning
going to watch basketball
Or volleyball or baseball
It's all fun
just leaves me a little
How should I say it
EXHAUSTED!

I want to keep doing it all
Teaching, learning, and attending sports
I think I just need a better way to do it
A better way of handling things
I write things down
that helps some
Its that reading that gets me, though
Those professors act like their textbooks are
some kind magnum opus

It would've fit fine in two paragraphs

Anyway, I'm outta here
I'm tired
Exhausted, if you will

Welcome Home

Heaven grants me
the stars as they show
their eyes to me,
piercing through the midnight sky
Twelve long hours ago
did I first depart from my dwelling
on a day's journey through life
and learning
and teaching
and loving as best as I can

When I left
the stars had been swallowed up by midnight
I had missed them
At this time however,
I see them all crystal clear
like diamonds
wrapped round the neck
of a beautiful woman
at a cocktail party
or the beads on a
hand-carved rosary
in the hands of a monk

They are there shining

to greet me
as I pull my feet ever so tiredly up the driveway
They are God's welcome
an invite into the warm embrace
of these four walls
"You are home now"
he says
"Rest"

Dally and Me

The Outsiders
S.E. Hinton
I've read it three times now
7th grade
10th grade
Sophomore in college
I was probably above that reading level the first time
let alone the third

I think about it alot every time I read it
Ponyboy and Johnny and staying gold and all that
But I really hit my pique interest with Dally
He's a misunderstood character if you ask me
I wonder if he would've been my friend
I wonder if I could've saved him

I would have let him stay on my couch
and smoke out back
or something
Anything to make the kid feel at home
I'd be the family he needed so desperately
I would take him under wing and say

“Listen, bud. You don’t need to keep running
around
getting into trouble. You got a home now.
I’ll hang with you
and help you with school.
I’ll be a brother.”

I wonder if I could have saved him
Hell, I wonder if I could save any of the Dally’s
of the world.

Horatio Alger: The Midwestern Father

Quit letting money
or bullies or school
or family history
get in the way of your destiny
Pull yourself up
by your own bootstraps
and make something of yourself

If you want to be a lawyer
than study your ass off in school
and get you a scholarship
Get yourself to a fine school
and study your ass off there
get you a law degree and
eat that bar exam for breakfast

If you want to be a doctor
Get that anatomy paper
down to memory
Study the bones
Study the organs
Hell, play operation for all I care
However you prep

Get yourself a med school degree
and become the MCATs worst nightmare

Look danger in the face
Take control of your future
and don't let it control you
Own it
Mold it
Hold it up for the whole damn generation to look
on
Make something of yourself, kid
Your the only one who can stop you

A Drop of Dew

Heaven's gates open wide
to drop a speck of dew
onto the canvas of the earth
The dew is a church
but yet seemingly dew compared to the galaxy
But the dew is rich in wonder
and beauty
In a place where many may not expect to find
beauty

It evokes awe in the faces of new patrons
Bringing them to their knees
at the presence of God
The Holy Spirit watches over all in the drop of
dew
Taking the place of both protector and peasant
Using heavens magic to lead the ill
whether physically or spiritually

I've been lead here
by a trail that I could not see
A yellow brick road
that held at the end much more than Dorothey
found
Redemption

Unwavering Love
Forgiveness
All in a drop of dew

I Read

I'm beginning to understand
The words don't just go in one ear
and out the other
like they used to
I don't mindlessly run my eyes
down every letter
like I used to

I read
I don't look
I don't scan
or scroll
I read
I read about the future
of children and education
and how the world as we know it
will shape the ones to come
I read about Holmes
solving riddles
that a hundred years later still baffle us
and turn us all into confused little Watsons

I don't just scan the names of Holmes
or Caulfield
I read

I meet them and get to know them
I let Palov tell me himself
how he trained little pooch so well
Just as Schrodinger explains that damn cat

I know long look
or scan
or scroll
I read
and soon enough I’ll understand

Water Tower

I love the water towers
that welcome people into small towns
They soar majestically above
the little one stoplight villages
Letting all who drive past
know that they are not to be looked down upon

They may be a tiny little town
in the middle of nowheresville, USA
but in this they take great pride
They take care of eachother
and look out for the vulnerable
It's really quite admirable
The watertower
Truly it is

Rainy Piano

Driving home from school
Rain beating my windshield
fogging my view
and my glasses
The collar on my jacket
itching me ever so slightly on the back of my
neck
I move steadily
45
down the Coliseum road

I'm comforted by the thought of my teacher
A brilliant scholar
of literature
describing the great wonders
and feats of the great writers
He is so calm
and yet so invested
in our minds

I'm distracted
or rather spirited away
by the piano
An instrument from decades past
Serenades me on my ride

as I ease my foot on and off the gas

Everybody loves a rainy piano
Ella's voice helps a lot too
I love the bustle of the day
At night, however, I need calm
The calming of reading or writing
or rain
or a piano

Blank Test

For the fourth time in a row
the paper is handed in
without so much as a name
But I know who it is
It can only be one person
her
it's always her

I don’t know why she does this
she is smart enough to figure this out
I would help
anyone of us would
Her friends, too

I don’t understand a blank test
I mean
at least guess
give it some kind of shot
You may be right
You never know

Probably not, though
you don’t pay any damn attention

Take Out the Trash

I can't think of another
person who enjoys
taking out the trash as much as I do
I don't know why
but for some reason
I just love wandering
up and down the driveway with that can
behind me
It gives me time to think about everything

I think about school
and how much or how little
homework I have
I think about my family
and how long it's been
since I've seen some of them
Or maybe I just pretend
to talk to my dog
She's a surprisingly
good conversationalist

I know it seems kind of
corny
but I just enjoy those five minutes off
where no one can touch me

No one can bother me
trying to sell me something
or themselves

Just me and the can
taking out the trash

www.ingramcontent.com/pod-product-compliance
Lightning Source LLC
Chambersburg PA
CBHW051738130826
49812CB00033B/907